I still love you, Dad

First published in this edition in 2010 by Evans Brothers Ltd
2A Portman Mansions
Chiltern Street
London W1U 6NR

Originally published in Belgium as Maar jij blijft mijn papa

British Library Cataloguing in Publication Data

Bode, Ann de.
   I still love you, dad. -- (Side by side)
   1. Children of separated parents--Juvenile fiction.
   2. Father and child--Juvenile fiction. 3. Separation
   (Psychology)--Juvenile fiction. 4. Children's stories.
   I. Title II. Series
   839.3'1364-dc22

ISBN-13: 9780237543044

Printed in China

Today is the school play!
Everyone is chatting and getting ready.
But Laura doesn't feel like joining in.

'What's the matter, Laura?' asks Tim.
'No one's coming to watch
me,' says Laura, crying.

Laura's dad has moved house.
Her mum and dad don't love
each other any more. Laura
lives with her mum and her
brother Thomas.

Laura misses her dad.
And she has to do more
jobs to help her mum.

When Laura stays with Dad, he gives her lots of presents. Laura doesn't want presents. She wants Dad to come back home.

'I know just how you feel,'
says Tim. His parents don't
live together either.
Laura starts to cheer up, and
gets ready for the play.

8

Now it's Tim's turn to look unhappy.
'You're thinking about your mum and dad
now, aren't you?' says Laura.
'Yes.'

The play is about to start. Laura
peeps through the curtains on stage.
Look – it's Mum!

And there's Dad, too.
Laura points to an empty
seat – next to Mum.
Perhaps they'll make up!
she thinks.

Laura is the star of the show.
She feels brave because she knows
Mum and Dad are watching.

12

Afterwards Mum says, 'You were wonderful!'
But where's Dad?
'He had to go,' says Mum.
Laura's happy feeling starts to disappear.

Back at home, Mum tells the children
to get ready for a visitor.
'Who's coming?' asks Laura, crossly.
'A new friend of mine,' says Mum. 'A man.'

Laura doesn't want a man to come round.
What will she say to him?
What if he's ugly or bald?
Or has a huge nose?

Thomas just says, 'Don't worry. It's nice
that Mum's got a new friend.'
'But what about Dad?' asks Laura.
'He's still our dad,' says Thomas.

16

Laura is cross and fed up.
I know! she thinks. I'll be so naughty
that this man won't want to be Mum's
friend any more!

17

Laura starts her plan straightaway.
'Take your feet off the table,' says Mum.
'OK,' says Laura, and takes off her shoes.
'Well you only said take my feet off,' she says.

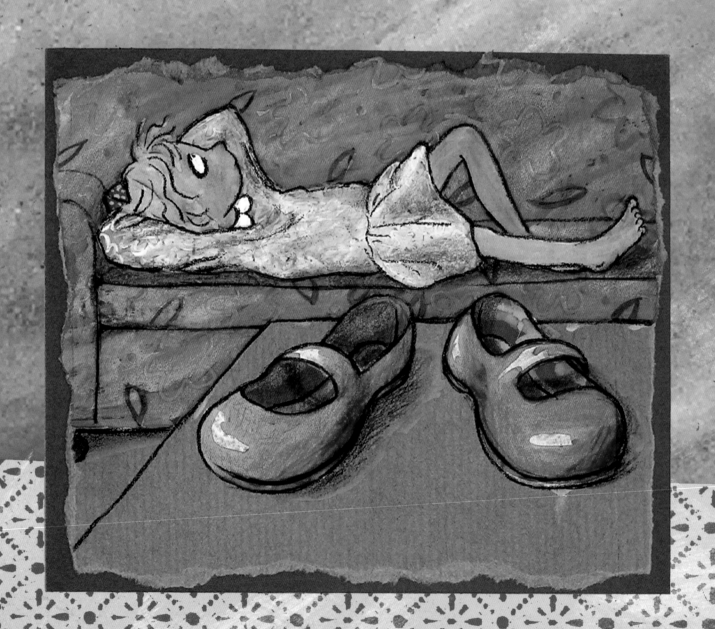

'Why do we have to have the posh tablecloth?' she asks rudely, and picks her nose.
'Stop that,' says Mum.

The visitor arrives.
'Laura, this is John,' says Mum.
Laura is surprised. He looks quite normal.
But she still doesn't like him.

When Mum goes out to the kitchen,
Laura pulls a silly face at John.
John just laughs and winks at her.

John looks at the books in the bookcase.
'We had lots more books when Dad
lived here,' says Laura.
'You must miss him,' says John.

'The table looks very smart,' says John.
'We always have it like this,' replies Laura.
'Quite right – fit for a little
princess like you.'

Slurp, slurp! Laura eats her soup noisily.
'Eat properly,' grumbles Mum.
Laura takes no notice.

John is sitting in Dad's place.
He shouldn't be there, thinks Laura.
But deep down she likes John.
She feels very confused. What about Dad?

Laura accidentally drops her cup.
Oh no! she thinks. Everything's gone wrong
since Mum and Dad split up.
Even her plot against John hasn't worked.

'Would you like any more?' asks Mum.
'No thanks,' says John. 'I'm full.'
'Huh! Dad could eat much more than you!
He'd have at least four helpings of
everything!' says Laura.

'Wow,' says John. 'I can't eat that much! But I can do this...'
He makes the spoon in his hand disappear... And then finds it behind Laura's ear – magic!

Oh no, look at the time! thinks Laura.
Her dad is about to pick her up.
He mustn't see John!
She runs to fetch her case.
'Is there a fire?' asks Mum.

The doorbell rings. It's Dad.
'Bye Mum,' says Laura.
'Say goodbye to John too,' says Mum.
'Goodbye John. Er... see you soon.'
And funnily enough, she hopes she will.

Laura doesn't know if she should
tell Dad about John.
But he asks her why she's so quiet.
'Mum had a visitor for tea – a man.'

Dad smiles and keeps on driving.
'That's good. Is he nice?' he asks.
'Umm... yes,' Laura says. 'But you'll
always be my dad.'